Forest Friends

Copyright © 2019 Ginger Nielson
All rights reserved
This is a coloring book for all ages, based upon
the naturе that surronds us.
No portion of this book may be copied in any form
whatsoever without the express written permission of the
author/illustrator, unless it is used as
an excerpt in a written review.
Contact: gingernielson@gmail.com

ISBN- 13: 978-0-578-50225-0
Printed in the United States of America
Ginger Nielson Children's Books

This book is dedicated to all who love the creatures of the forest and beyond.
And it is for all those who support and help to preserve those lives.

WHAT ARE WE CALLED?

Welcome to the forest! In this book you will find many of the animals you already know so well. On the other hand, although they live in the forest, there may be some new animals for you to find.

Each animal is painted on one page and on the opposite page is a line drawing for you to color. You can use any color and even change the look of an animal to suit your style.

What do you call the animal in a group? The names of each group are printed on the colored page. These are fun names to remember.

It is a good idea to use colored pencils or sharp crayons so that the colors don't bleed through to the next page.

Happy coloring, happy reading and happy hunting.

Have fun with the book; share with friends.

WHAT DO YOU SEE?

Out of the forest and into the night
come creatures that scurry, creep and take flight.

Fur, feathers, claws, and scales, quite unique
help them to crouch, hunt and quietly seek.

Climbing and dancing and quickly they run,
until they are warned by the first rays of sun.

Then back to the forest 'til the end of the day
resting in dens, hollow logs, and soft hay.

Some friends are out the whole day long,
filling the air with color and song.

Wings and tails and slugs and snails,
come to the garden until the light fails.

But all these creatures are always near by,
ready to pounce, hunt, sing, chase, and fly.

A Herd of Deer

An Orchestra of Crickets

A Pack of Coyotes

A Herd of Bobcats

A Sloth of Bears

A Sneak of Weasels

A Surfeit of Skunk

A Congregation of Rook

A Prickle of Porcupines

A Nest of Mice

A Hover of Hummingbirds

These two pages are for you. Make notes of what you see in the forest near you, or just in your own yard. Maybe you will draw some pictures here too.
If you want to send me any of your drawings, I would love to see them. You can E-mail them to me at:
gingernielson@gmail.com

More than anything else, I want you to have fun with this book~

www.ingramcontent.com/pod-product-compliance
Lightning Source LLC
Chambersburg PA
CBRC092338290426
44108CB00008B/139